There are five candles in ou
but my favourite is the talles

The candle flame helps us think about
Jesus. We say he is like a light.

There are many different
stories told about Jesus.
At Christmas we hear
stories about how
he was born.

G000055027

A very long time ago there was a woman called Mary. An angel visited her and told her that she was going to have a special baby.

She was really frightened at first but the angel told her not to be afraid.

Then the angel said that Mary's baby was going to be a very special baby. He would be God's Son!

Mary was amazed but she knew that her baby was going to be someone special.

When Mary was about to have her baby, she and Joseph had to go on a long journey. They had to travel to Joseph's old home in Bethlehem.

At Bethlehem they needed somewhere to sleep. It was so busy that the only place they could find was a stable, next to an inn.

5

The special baby was born in the stable. Mary and Joseph did not have a cot, so they wrapped him up warmly and laid him in the food trough!

They did not give him his name for a whole week, but Mary knew all the time that he was to be called Jesus because the angel had told her so.

Her baby was a special baby.

There were some shepherds in the fields. Suddenly lots of angels appeared. The shepherds were very frightened, just like Mary.

The angels told them the good news about the special baby. They rushed to see him. When they told Mary and Joseph their story they were all amazed.

Mary thought about all these things. Her baby really was a special baby!

Some time later, wise men, called Magi, saw a new star shining like a bright candle. They thought it was the sign of a new-born king, so they followed it to the palace.

King Herod was worried. He did not want someone else to be king in his country. So he said to the men, "Come back and tell me what you find."

The wise men found the baby Jesus. They bowed down before him and gave him gifts of gold, frankincense and myrrh.

Mary and Joseph were amazed at all the visitors who came to see their special baby.

The wise men went home a different way because they realised that King Herod would try to kill Jesus.

After this, Mary and Joseph realised that Jesus was in danger. So they took him on a long journey to Egypt, where they knew he would be safe.

They stayed in Egypt until they knew it was safe to return home.

Mary and Joseph were sure that God had special plans for this baby.

13

Christmas Day is Jesus' birthday. In church on the four Sundays before Christmas, we light the red candles on our Advent ring. We light one more red candle each week.

On Christmas Day we light the tallest candle. We think that Jesus is like a light. Just as a light helps you see in the darkness, so Jesus helps us see more of what God is like.

We sing carols, share presents and celebrate this happy day.

Can you tell
a story about
Christmas?

Published by Religious and Moral Education Press, A division of SCM-Canterbury Press Ltd, St Mary's Works, St Mary's Plain, Norwich, Norfolk NR3 3BH

Copyright © 1999 Lynne Broadbent and John Logan. Lynne Broadbent and John Logan have asserted their right under the Copyright, Designs and Patents Act, 1988, to be identified as Authors of this Work.

All rights reserved. First published 1999. ISBN 1 85175 184 X

Designed and typeset by Topics – The Creative Partnership, Exeter. Printed in Great Britain by Brightsea Press, Exeter for SCM-Canterbury Press Ltd, Norwich